PAINTING
GLASS

STEP-BY-STEP CRAFTS

PAINTING GLASS

CAROLINE GREEN

CREATIVE
PUBLISHING
international

MINNETONKA, MINNESOTA

First published in the USA and Canada by
Creative Publishing international, Inc.

5900 Green Oak Drive
Minnetonka, MN 55343
1-800-328-3895

Published in United Kingdom by
New Holland Publishers (UK) Ltd

Published in 2000 by
New Holland Publishers (UK) Ltd
London • Cape Town • Sydney • Auckland

ISBN 0-86573-167-5

Editor: Tessa Clark
Designer: Grahame Dudley
Photographer: John Freeman
Assistant Editor: Anke Ueberberg

Editorial Direction: Rosemary Wilkinson

10 9 8 7 6 5 4 3 2 1

Reproduction by
PICA Colour Separation, Singapore
Printed and bound in Malaysia by
Times Offset (M) Sdn. Bhd.

Contents

Introduction *6*

Getting Started *8*

PROJECTS

1: Molded Bottles and Jars *18*

2: Stained Glass Night Lights *22*

3: Perfume Bottles *26*

Bottles and Vases Gallery *30*

4: Tumblers and Coasters *32*

5: Lightcatchers *36*

Glasses Gallery *40*

6: Square Flower Vases *42*

7: Hurricane Lamp *46*

8: Blue and Gold Glassware *50*

Flora and Fauna Gallery *54*

9: Candle and Tea-light Holders *56*

10: Swedish-style Wine Glasses *60*

Lightcatchers Gallery *64*

11: Rainbow Jug, Tumblers and Bowls *66*

12: Flowery Salad Plates and Bowl *70*

Mirrors, Frames and Candle

Holders Gallery *74*

13: Roman Vase *76*

14: Beaded Blind *80*

Plates and Bowls Gallery *84*

15: Art Deco Uplight *86*

Templates *92*

Suppliers and Acknowledgements *95*

Index *96*

Introduction

The history of glass is a fascinating subject dating back to early Egyptian times. Several projects in this book pay homage to historical pieces, from ancient Etruscan flasks to gold-painted Venetian designs. Floral painted glass was very popular in eastern Europe, as was the glowing mediaeval stained glass in Britain; subtle etched glass was a favorite in eighteenth-century Sweden. All of these styles can be imitated using modern products. It is also possible to create fashionable frosted glass items using paints and sprays to decorate the surface.

Painting glass is a most enjoyable and fruitful hobby. You will find it can be both a restful pastime and an outlet for your artistic leanings! You'll see that many projects only need a steady hand to make lines of dots and dashes in glowing colors which will produce surprisingly attractive designs for all sorts of glassware. As you get more experienced, your talents will expand from painting simple flowers and patterns to designing and painting your own glassware. Follow the styles that you like and collect pictures and examples of other glassware to use as reference. Soon you'll be able to paint whole sets of glassware and even wineglasses to match your china. You'll find yourself painting glass for your own home, for presents and perhaps even for sale at craft fairs!

This craft can begin in a very small way, perhaps with the gift of a craft kit or a voucher. You can choose a small range of three or four colors and one or two brushes to get you going and then the sky's the limit. I started by decorating empty jam jars and mineral water bottles, progressed to junk shop finds and then, as my confidence grew, I purchased a few special items to make sets of designer-style glasses, bowls, vases and plates. In fact, wherever I looked, there were things made of glass that could be decorated. Try mirrors, clip frames and window panes when ordinary glassware seems too easy!

The production of new paints like Pébéo's Porcelaine 150 means that you can now paint lasting designs on everyday glassware. Even better, the paints are safe in contact with food and drink and dishwasher-proof.

This book is aimed at satisfying the needs of people of all levels of ability. It gives all the advice and up-to-date information you will need to choose the right products and learn the basic and the more advanced techniques of painting on glass, and the projects and galleries will provide fresh ideas and further inspiration for both the novice and the more experienced glass painter.

I have found that putting together these ideas, painting the glass and writing the instructions has been a really exciting task, and I hope that the readers of this book will find my efforts both inspiring and instructive, but above all, enjoyable.

Caroline Green

Caroline Green

Getting Started

GLASSWARE

There are endless opportunities to find glassware for painting. Go for interesting shapes, one-off pieces, antique finds or something totally modern. Hunt out bargains on market stalls or in secondhand or charity shops and rediscover forgotten favorites hidden at the back of your cupboards. Buy inexpensive wine goblets, glass bowls or jugs and paint them in the latest styles for a designer look. Even a humble jam jar can be transformed into an eye-catching accessory!

Garage sales are ideal hunting grounds for bargains, and don't forget sale time in your favorite department stores. Look for glass in all its different forms, from a simple tumbler to more unusual plates, vases and empty bottles. Mirrors, clip frames and even window glass and glass doors in furniture are also good subjects for painting. Both clear and colored glass can be decorated and you can paint onto frosted glass or create your own frosting. To make lightcatchers or coasters, order the sizes you need from a glass-cutting shop or buy ready-made shapes from arts and crafts stores.

Virtually anything made of glass can be used for a project that you will enjoy doing, and that will give you a beautiful end result.

Make sure your glassware is clean. Wash old, dirty items in hot water and detergent, then rinse them in clean hot water. Leave them to drain, then dry with a clean tea towel. Even new glass should be washed and dried carefully to remove grease and dirt.

When you are ready to paint, always degrease the surface of the glass. Rub denatured alcohol onto it with a lint-free cloth, then leave to dry. This will ensure that the paint adheres properly to the glass.

EQUIPMENT

Brushes

There are so many different brushes on the market that the experienced hobbyist as well as the beginner can become confused. Always use watercolor brushes for the liquid paints used in glass painting.

There are two types of brushes: made from natural sable or squirrel hair, and from various synthetic fibers. Natural hair is the best, and the most expensive, but synthetic fibers come a very close second and are much cheaper.

Continuous use of solvents will reduce the life of both kinds of fibers so it is advisable to buy the least expensive ones for use with oil-based paints. Brushes come in a variety of shapes and their uses are dealt with in detail on page 13.

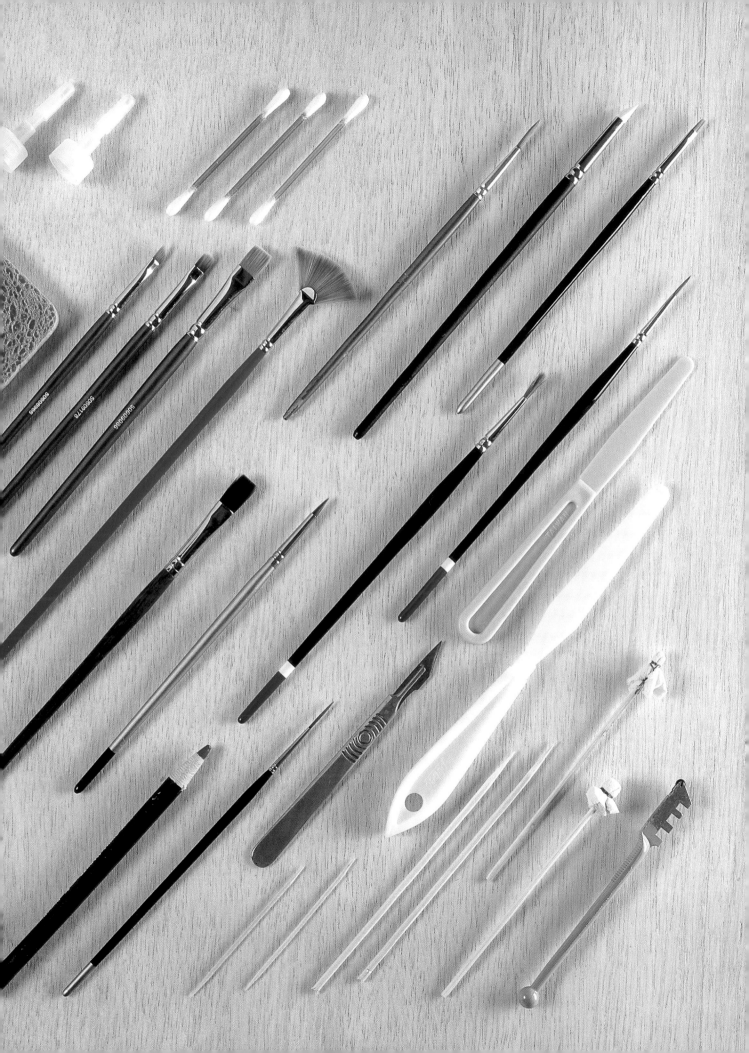

Palette knives and spatulas
It is best to use plastic versions of these as they will not scratch the surface of the glass and can be washed easily. They are also less expensive than metal ones.

Chinagraph (colored wax) pencil
A colored wax pencil is useful for marking positions on glass as its greasy texture adheres to the shiny surface. You can buy the pencils in different colors so that they show up on different colored shiny surfaces. Always clean off the marks with a cotton bud dipped in denatured alcohol before painting or the paint may not adhere properly to the glass.

Masking tape
This low-tack tape is very useful for covering areas of glass so that you can create bold stencilled designs. You can also use it to attach traced patterns to the glass and when you are using acetate stencils. To measure and plan formal designs and position them accurately on a curved shape like a wine glass or vase, press a strip of masking tape around its rim, cut it to the circumference of the rim, then remove it and mark the positions for the motifs you will be using. Press the tape around the rim again and use the marks as a guide for your painting.

Craft knife or scalpel
A sharp, pointed craft knife or scalpel will enable you to cut accurately and cleanly when you are making a stencil or trimming masking tape to make patterns. It is also useful for removing stray spots of dried paint from glass.

Sponges
Both natural sea sponges and synthetic sponges are ideal for applying glass paints over a large area and for creating a mottled texture in the paint. Use a natural sponge for a more open, bold texture and a synthetic version for a fine one.

Cotton buds and sponge applicators
Cotton buds and sponge applicators can be used to apply paint in the form of regular round dots and also to remove mistakes.

Cocktail sticks and wooden skewers
Use cocktail sticks or wooden skewers to scratch designs into wet paint and to hold painted beads while they are drying.

Glass cutter
A glass cutter will enable you to score and break simple glass shapes from thin glass for fitting into picture frames or for making lightcatchers with cord around the edges. However, if you are making coasters or similar items with unprotected edges you will need to get the edges ground to a smooth finish.

PAINTS, SPRAYS AND GELS

There is an ever-increasing choice of glass painting products, ranging from traditional, solvent- and water-based paints in transparent and opaque finishes to frosting sprays, outliners and gels. Start by buying a few colors in one or two of these categories to get the feel of how to use them and build up your confidence.

Oil-based paints
Oil-based paints such as Vitrail produce a wonderfully clear, glossy finish with colors that glow when held up to the light. They will give the genuine look of stained glass, particularly when combined with dark outliners. The colors work best when applied in small areas using a round brush. They are only suitable for decorative pieces such as lightcatchers, vases, mirrors and clip frames as they need to be washed carefully and infrequently in cool water. These paints can also be used for the random marbling technique described on page 16.

Leave the item flat while it dries so that the color does not run. The paints are mostly transparent and will dry quite quickly (a thin coat will be touch-dry in about 10 minutes) so replace the lids of the pots carefully to prevent the paints from evaporating. Leave the finished item to dry for 48 hours before using it.

Clean brushes in thinners or mineral spirits, then wash them in a solution of warm water and detergent.

Water-based paints
Water-based paints such as Pébéo Porcelaine 150 are primarily for use on china but they work very well on glassware, giving a permanent form of decoration when they are fired in a domestic oven. They are completely safe after baking and so can be used on tableware and glasses. Apply them with a brush or sponge to create transparent and semi-opaque designs. There is a wide range of colors and they can be mixed with each other to create new shades. They can also be made paler by diluting them with filler undercoat. To deepen the color, leave the first coat to dry for 10 minutes then apply a second coat. The paints have a glossy finish when dry, but if you require a matte finish you can add matte medium before applying them.

The paints will be touch-dry in about one hour and completely dry in 24 hours. To bake the colors, leave to dry for at least 24 hours then place the glassware in a cold oven and set

the temperature to 150°C/300°F. When the oven reaches this temperature, bake the glassware for 35 minutes. Then switch off the oven and allow it to cool before removing the glass. The oven temperature must be correct. If glassware is fired at a lower temperature, the paint will not harden sufficiently to become permanent. At a higher temperature the paint will become permanent but the colors may darken.

It is possible to correct mistakes before firing by wiping off the error with a cotton bud soaked in water. Wash brushes out in clean water.

Water-based paints that simulate the look of stained glass include Gallery Glass™ products, available in a variety of colors, in a clear formula, and in black to simulate leading. The paints come in squeeze bottles with long nozzles for easy application direct from the bottle. The leading paint must dry for 24 hours before applying the colors adjacent to it. The colors and clear formula dry to a textured, transparent finish in about 24 hours. The paints can easily be washed from the glass surface with water while wet, or peeled from the glass when dry. These paints are not appropriate for items that frequently come in contact with water and should not be used on items that come in contact with food. However, with easy cleanup and removal, they are appropriate for seasonal designs and simple craft items.

Gel paints

Gel paints, such as Pébéo Gel Crystal, come in transparent, iridescent and opaque types, all of which dry to a glossy finish. They can be applied straight from the tube onto the glass, then spread out with a palette knife or brush or directed in narrow lines with a nozzle to create unusual three-dimensional effects. They can also be used to imitate blown glass effects. While the gels are still wet you can embed items such as glass nuggets, sequins, shells, metallic threads and beads in them to create jewelry and highly original pieces of glassware; or you can scrape patterns into them with a plastic spatula or a comb made of card. You can also use them for stencilling, combine them with outliner for Tiffany glass effects or create a dimpled, frosted effect by applying opaline gels with a sponge.

The gels will be touch-dry in 30 minutes and the thickest layer will take up to a week to dry.

Wash brushes and palette knives in water.

Water-based enamel paints

Water-based, transparent enamel paints, such as Pébéo Liquid Crystal paints, have a glossy finish when dry and allow you to achieve beautiful flat washes without brush marks. The paints can be diluted with water for a pastel effect and you can achieve frosted colors by combining the paints with matte varnish, such as Liquid Crystal. Colors can be mixed to create new shades.

The paints will be touch-dry in about 20 minutes and fully dry in two or three days.

Wash brushes out in water.

Matte varnish and matte medium

Both these products can be painted onto glass with a brush or sponged directly through a stencil for an opaque frosted effect. The varnish helps to stop colors fading and will be touch-dry in 20 minutes and completely dry in two to three days. The matte medium becomes dishwasher-proof when baked and is slightly thicker than the varnish, so it is more suitable for stencilling. It will be touch-dry in 10 minutes and must be left to dry for 24 hours before baking as described for Porcelaine 150 paints.

For both products, wash brushes out in clean water.

Frosting or glass etch spray

This provides a fast way to create fashionable, frosted glass effects for decorative purposes and is ideal for use with stencil designs and on windows and mirrors as well as vases or display dishes. However, it is not suitable for items that will need frequent washing. It comes in a limited range of pastel shades and also as a colorless frosting.

The spray will be touch-dry in 5 to 10 minutes and completely dry in an hour.

Clean off any overspray with a cotton bud dipped in mineral spirits.

Outliners

Cern relief outliners are water-based and come in a tube with a long, thin nozzle. It takes a little practice to become proficient in their use, but once you are, they have great design potential. They produce a line of a consistent width which allows you to follow patterns, and make outlines or dot patterns that can be used on their own or added to painted designs. Simple outliners come in several colors as well as metallic shades and can be baked in the oven.

Outlined shapes should be dry enough for you to color in the rest of the item with paint after about 20 minutes, but you must be careful not to smudge them. I find it easier to speed up the process by placing the object in a very low oven and waiting until the lines are hard before painting in colors to complete a design. Both products will be completely dry in 24 hours. Bake the outliner as described for Porcelaine 150 paints.

BASIC TECHNIQUES

Painting with a round brush

A round watercolor brush will hold the maximum amount of paint and also has a point for detailed work. You will find that it is the most useful brush in your collection, with many sizes available in both natural and synthetic fibers. Large sizes will produce a beautiful flat wash and will cover large areas quickly, but for detailed work choose a much smaller size with a fine point. Round brushes are ideal for filling in outline designs as they allow you to paint right up to the line and so avoid gaps in the color, and make an even wash without creating bubbles in the paint.

Painting with a flat brush

A flat watercolor brush is ideal for painting stripes, zigzags and patterns that depend on wider lines of a uniform thickness. Choose a width of brush slightly narrower than the line you want to make. Use the brush flat to create thick lines, or at an angle, like an italic pen, for thinner ones. You can also use it to make square dots that can form the basis of a variety of different patterns. We used this simple, easy technique for the rainbow design on page 66.

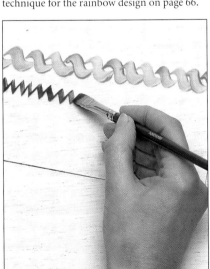

Painting with a long-haired brush

A thin, round watercolor brush with extra-long fibers is used to great effect for painting both straight and wavy lines. Because the brush is so fine you can only use it to paint lines of a certain width, which helps to keep the pattern even. It will hold quite a good amount of paint, so you can paint a long way with one stroke. Plant stems and tendrils are best painted using these brushes, and abstract line patterns also work well with them.

Painting with a fan-shaped brush

A fan-shaped watercolor brush is one of the more unusual brushes to have in your collection but it can be most useful for a specific project. Used flat, as shown here, it will produce a soft, cloudy texture which is perfect for naturalistic designs – it will look just like distant grass, water, sky or sand, depending on the colors chosen. It is also good for covering a large area with a gentle texture, which is sometimes difficult to achieve. Used on the edge of an item, it will highlight its outline and emphasize its shape or create an attractive, soft-edged frame for your design.

Painting with an angled brush

An angled watercolor brush is basically the same as a flat brush, but the ends of the fibers are cut off at an angle. With this brush, it is easy to make simple diamond shapes that are very effective for formal patterns, and with a little practice you will be able to make natural-looking leaves and petals for delightful floral designs. The leaf shown here is worked in two strokes. To make narrower leaves and daisy-type petals, dab the end of the brush onto the surface in one stroke to make a perfect shape each time. Try this with the daisy design on page 70.

Sponging with a natural sponge

Sponging is a quick way to color a large area. Depending on the openness of the sponge, you can make a boldly textured pattern or create a fine speckled effect. Try applying a second coat when the first one has dried for a more solid color, or blend two or more colors, without mixing the paint on a palette, by gradually overlapping the different shades.

Always wet a natural sponge and squeeze

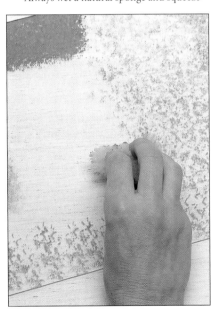

out all the moisture to make the sponge soft and pliable before using paint. Then pour a little paint onto a palette and dip just the tip of the sponge into it. Dab off the excess paint on scrap paper or the side of the palette, then work on the glass with a light dabbing motion. Dab off the excess every time you replenish the paint on the sponge to keep the texture even and avoid unsightly blobs.

Natural sponges are quite expensive so if you want them to last as long as possible use only water-based paints and rinse them out in warm water as soon as possible after use. However, they are also suitable for oil-based paints if you clean them with mineral spirits immediately after you've finished painting and then rinse them thoroughly in warm water and detergent.

All-over sponging with a synthetic foam sponge

A synthetic foam sponge is cheaper than a natural one and creates a finer-textured effect. You can blend colors in the same way and achieve a darker-shaded effect by pressing more heavily. Cut a sponge into small cubes with scissors. To imitate the texture of a natural sponge you can pull tiny pieces out of the surface of a cube to change its square outline and regular finish. Simply throw the cubes of sponge away when you have finished painting.

Painting with cotton buds

Working with cotton buds is a cross between drawing and painting. The cotton tip soaks up the paint so that it is remarkably easy to control. Each cotton bud will only last for a short time. When the tip gets too worn and enlarged, simply use a fresh one.

Start by using cotton buds to make rows of wonderfully uniform round dots, then progress to multicolored patterns,

incorporating stripes and squiggles. You can build up exciting designs in this way, then just throw away the cotton buds at the end.

Sponging with a foam applicator

This method is very similar to the cotton bud technique but the resulting dots are larger and each applicator will last for a complete job. To make one, cut a thin sponge kitchen cloth into small squares and place the tip of a wooden skewer in the center of a square. Gather the sponge around the tip of the skewer, then bind it with a piece of thin wire to make a rounded, spongy end.

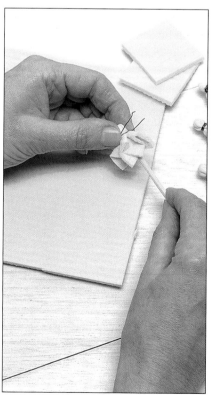

Stencilling

To stencil a design, use your own stencil or a ready-cut one and spray the reverse of the film with stencil mount. Leave this for a few minutes until it becomes tacky, then press the stencil in position on the glass. Using stencil mount is particularly useful on curved sufaces as it stops the stencil slipping. Using a piece of

synthetic sponge, dab the color over the stencil. Do not use too much paint as it may seep under the edges of the film.

When you are happy with the paint coverage, lift off the stencil carefully to reveal the pattern. Continue in this way to complete the design, then leave until the paint is completely dry. If there are any stray bits of paint around the edges of the design, scrape these off with the tip of a craft knife.

Masking shapes for sponging

You can use masking tape to make effective one-off patterns on your glassware. Lengths of tape can be used to delineate straight edges, or can be torn to produce uneven shapes. Simply press in place where you want the glass to remain clear.

When you have masked your whole design, sponge color lightly into the spaces around or between the tape. Use any type of glass paint and aim for a light, even coverage.

Leave until touch-dry, then carefully peel off the tape to reveal the patterns. If some of

the paint starts to peel off along with the tape, it is probably because you have left it too long before removing the tape and the paint has formed a hard film. To keep the edge neat, run the tip of a craft knife along the edge of the tape before continuing to peel it off.

Scratching designs into wet color

After painting or sponging on a layer of flat color you can add a decorative element by scratching designs into the paint down to the surface of the glass while the paint is still wet. Try using a plastic spatula to create sharp lines and swirls.

Use the tip of a cotton bud to make stripes, zigzags and dots. To keep the pattern well defined, change the cotton bud when it becomes saturated with paint.

The point of a cocktail stick or wooden skewer makes fine, detailed patterns and can even be used for writing. Wipe the tip on clean tissue paper every now and then to remove excess paint.

Using outliner

Unscrew the nozzle and pierce the top of the tube, then quickly replace the nozzle. Squeeze the tube very gently to bring the paint to the tip of the nozzle, wipe the tip on a tissue, then begin to draw. It is best to perfect the technique by practicing on a piece of glass or acetate, or on an old jam jar, before working on your glassware. Touch the paint to the glass, then lift the nozzle very slightly to draw the line of paint along. Let the paint fall onto the glass so that it forms an even line rather than dragging the nozzle along the surface of the glass, which will produce an untidy line. The method is similar to using an icing bag to pipe decorative piping onto a cake. Practice following traced outlines to form perfect shapes. It is very easy to make a wiggly all-over pattern, as on the perfume bottles on page 26. Simply let your hand follow a natural, wavy pattern, then repeat this until the surface is evenly covered.

You can also make tiny dots to embellish an outline or decorate a simple pattern. Simply touch the tip of the nozzle to the glass and lift it off sharply. Do not squeeze the tube hard as too much paint will come out, and keep a tissue handy to wipe the tip frequently to keep it clean. If you make a mistake, wait for about 10 minutes until the paint has hardened slightly, then simply scrape it off the glass with the tip of a craft knife.

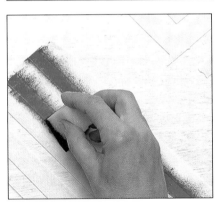

Etching or frosting designs

Clear matte medium can be used to great effect to create subtle, frosted patterns. You can paint it on with a brush to make detailed patterns or simple stripes, or sponge it on through a stencil. The frosting will become even as it dries, until it is completely uniform.

Spray frosting can also be used with stencils or to cover a complete surface. Shake the aerosol can and then spray the item lightly from a short distance away. Aim for a light, even coating and leave until touch-dry before repeating the process. Continue in this way until you achieve the desired level of frosting.

Using gels
Clear and opaque water-based gels can be built up on glass to create thick, three-dimensional effects for a modern look. It is an easy process that requires minimal artistic skill and is fun to do. Apply the gel straight from the tube, randomly onto the glass, and use a brush, sponge or palette knife to spread it out over the surface. To make patterns, drag a comb made from card across the wet gel.

Use a nozzle screwed onto the end of the tube of gel to make lines. Squeeze the tube evenly and pipe the gel onto the surface. Clean the nozzle when necessary. You can also use the nozzle to create rows of small dots, and for larger blobs that can be used instead of glue to anchor glass nuggets.

Use a palette knife to spread blobs of gel so that they cover the surface. You can easily alter the density of the color by making the layer of gel thinner or, for a deeper shade, letting it form thick ridges.

Glueing on nuggets, beads, sequins or shells
As well as painting glassware you can also glue embellishments to the surface using a special glass-bonding adhesive. This cures in sunlight to form a secure, clear bond. Glass nuggets, sequins, beads and shells can all be used for exciting three-dimensional effects on otherwise plain or ordinary pieces. The added jewels will give your glassware a rich and sumptuous look.

To use glass adhesive, put a tiny blob of glue on the back of the embellishment you have chosen, then press it in place. Lay the

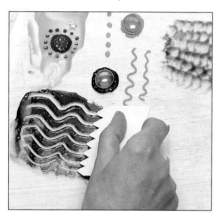

item flat in direct sunlight until the glue has hardened. The glue will also harden in daylight, without sun, but more slowly. You can use a glue gun for decorating larger objects, but the adhesive may be more visible.

Creating a crackle finish
Create an antique look by finishing off with a crackle glaze. Paint the glass with a layer of water-based enamel paint or gloss anti-UV varnish and leave until touch-dry. Then use a medium-sized, round watercolor brush to paint quickly over this with a fairly thick coat of crackling medium. Paint in one direction, with as few brush strokes as possible, then leave to dry and form a matte, crackle finish. This will take 1 to 4 hours, depending on the

thickness of the coat you have applied. You can speed up the process and increase the crackling by using a hairdryer: hold it about 15 cm (6 in) away from the surface. A crackle finish gives a fairly random effect and the results depend on the thickness of the coat of crackling medium and the speed of the drying time, so it is wise to experiment before trying the technique out on your glass.

Marbling on glass
Use oil-based glass paints, such as Vitrail, to make a fantasy marbled finish. Find a container slightly larger than your chosen piece of glass and half-fill it with water. Using the tip of a cocktail stick or a dropper, flick drops of two or three different colors onto the surface of the water. Some drops will spread thinly and others will form random shapes. Swirl the colors about gently to mingle them, then quickly dip the glass item into the water to pick up the paint on the surface before it dries. Lift the item out cleanly and leave it to dry, without disturbing the paint. Repeat the process to deepen the colors, fill any gaps and add different shades. When the paint is dry, add gold or a differently colored edging for a more formal style.

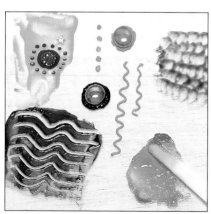

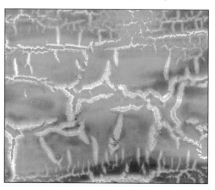

DESIGN
INSPIRATION

As well as the designs in this book you will find many other sources of inspiration just waiting to be used and adapted to glass painting. Greeting cards, wrapping paper, wallpaper, fabrics, advertisements, brochures and magazine features are all excellent. Start to collect scraps that will become the beginnings of your own, unique style. The shape or color of a piece of glass often

suggests a suitable design and the intended use for the item may help you decide on a theme. Use copyright-free design books for reference and trace, or photocopy, outlines of your favorite designs. Try out different color schemes. Enlarge a single motif for the central part of a design on a photocopier and work out repeat patterns to use on borders or on matching pieces of glassware.

Changing colorways
Try out different colorways to realize a design's full potential. For example, the simple leaf-and-dot design (below) looks like springtime mimosa blossom when it is colored in moss green and yellow with a little blue. Try to achieve a different effect by re-coloring it in red and emerald green, and it becomes the perfect Christmas border design.

Molded Bottles and Jars

Molded bottles and jars come in all shapes and sizes and can be purchased quite cheaply. Decorating them makes an excellent first project if you've never done any glass painting before, as you don't need to draw a design on the glass. The idea is to follow the molded lines and patterns rather like coloring in an outline drawing. You can choose naturalistic colors or pick a fantasy scheme of three or four toning shades. We used a bottle with a grapevine pattern in this project, but the technique can be applied to any molded design. Salad oils and vinegars look particularly good in painted bottles.

You will need

chartreuse
pink
emerald
lemon
green gold
violet

A bottle with a
molded design
Small round brushes
Transparent
glass paints
Fine pointed brushes
Appropriate thinner
for cleaning brushes

1 Clean the bottle thoroughly. Using the round brush, paint over a leaf in emerald. Follow the outline and then fill in the center. Work fairly quickly and use enough paint to cover the area easily without leaving brush marks. Continue painting until all the leaves on this side of the bottle are filled in.

2 To achieve a very naturalistic look, shade a single leaf with two colors. Leave some of the leaf free of the emerald and use a clean brush to introduce the green-gold while the emerald is still wet. Continue in this way until all the leaves are colored. Leave to dry, then work on the other side of the item.

3 Paint each fruit in the bunch of grapes individually with a circular motion, using the violet. Although this takes longer than painting the bunch as one area, it will look more natural and avoid a messy finish. You can leave a tiny space at the center of each grape to look like natural shine as shown below. Leave to dry.

artist's tip

If paint accidentally goes over the edge of the molded design, wipe it away quickly with a clean cotton bud before it dries.

4 Use the fine pointed brush to paint in the narrow stems and tendrils and the veins in the leaves. Work carefully after the other colors have dried, to avoid smudging. Leave to dry, then work on the opposite side of the bottle in the same way.

artist's tip

If you find that parts of a molded design are difficult to see when you are painting, push some white tissue inside the jar or bottle to help you.

5 Paint the veins when the main leaf area is completely dry so that you retain the fine detail. When coloring the veins on the leaves, use the chartreuse, which contrasts well with the color of the leaf.

Alternative design:

Abstract pattern

When painting bottles that have an abstract pattern, choose a range of three or four colors to build up the design. You do not need to color in all the areas — spaces can often add to the overall effect and complement your chosen colors.

P aint empty jam jars to make safe and pretty night-light holders that look enchanting on a window-sill or mantelpiece. If you add a secure wire loop they can also be hung from shelves — or from the branches of trees for alfresco events.

Safety note: Never leave lighted candles unattended.

You will need

yellow
crimson
relief outliner in black

Empty jam jars
Lighter fluid (optional)
Relief outliner
Small round brushes
Transparent
glass paints
Palette
Appropriate thinner
Night lights
Wire for hanging
(optional)

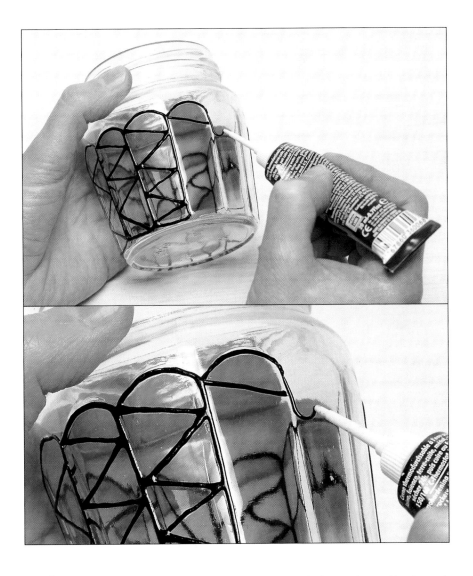

1 Clean the jars thoroughly. If necessary, remove any sticky residue left by the labels with lighter fluid. Using the black outliner, draw a freehand crazy paving design on the outside of one of the jars, taking care not to smudge the lines as you work. (If you make a mistake, wipe it off quickly with a damp cloth.) Leave to dry.

PROJECT

2

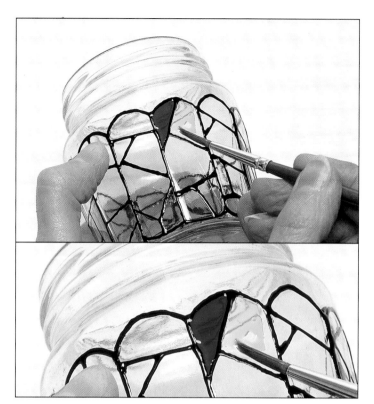

2 Dip a brush into the crimson paint and apply a thin, even layer of color in one of the shapes on the jar. Work with the jar on its side so that the paint does not run. Then use a clean brush to apply yellow to the shape next to it.

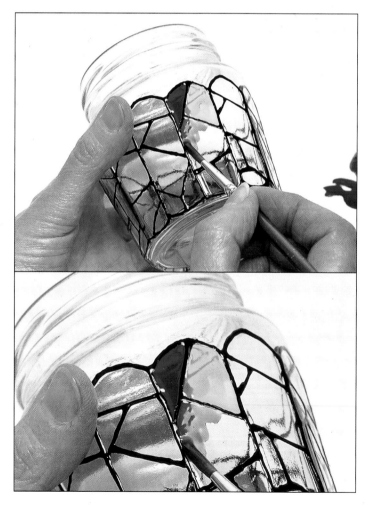

3 Gradually work around the jar filling in all the areas with a range of colors: try mixing the paints together to make lots of different shades.

artist's tip

When you have finished painting, clean your brushes in the thinner, then rinse them in soapy water and shake off excess moisture. Wrap them in absorbent kitchen paper and leave to dry. This will preserve their shape and the condition of their fibers.

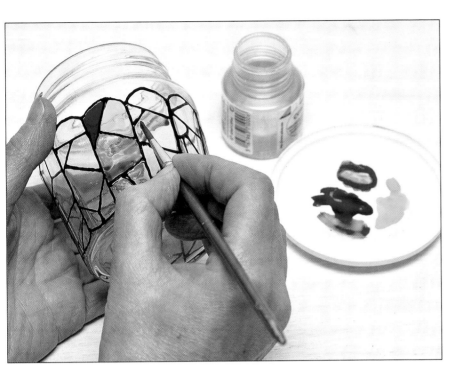

This painted design creates a pretty stained glass effect when the night lights inside the jars are lit.

4 You can mix the paints with a little of the clear thinners to create much paler shades. If you want deeper shades, allow the first, unthinned, coat to dry and then apply a second one.

artist's tip
When you are working on a round object, lay it on its side to dry. This will prevent the paint running from one area into the next. Stop it from rolling about by supporting it with pieces of kneadable adhesive.

5 Leave the jar until the paint is completely dry, then place a night light inside it. Tie a length of wire securely around the top of the jar and make a loop if you wish to hang the light up.

R ich gold outliner and miniature jewelled stickers turn
these colored perfume bottles into luxury accessories
for the bathroom or dressing table. Tie with extravagant
organdie ribbon bows or tassels to complete the effect.

You will need

outliner in gold

Small colored bottles
with stoppers
Denatured alcohol
Outliner, as above
A pack of decorative
stickers
Tweezers
Glass bond adhesive
Organdie ribbon or
tassels to decorate

1 Clean the
outside of
the bottles
with denatured
alcohol to make sure
the glass is grease-
free, and remember
to hold them at the
top and bottom
while painting.
Squeeze the gold
outliner into the tip
of the nozzle and
start to draw a
natural, flowing,
wiggly design on the
shoulder area of one
of the bottles. Work
from just under the
neck downward.

2 Continue in this way until you have created a richly patterned area that comes about halfway down the bottle. Leave small, randomly spaced areas without paint to decorate later with the stickers. Leave the outliner to dry until hard.

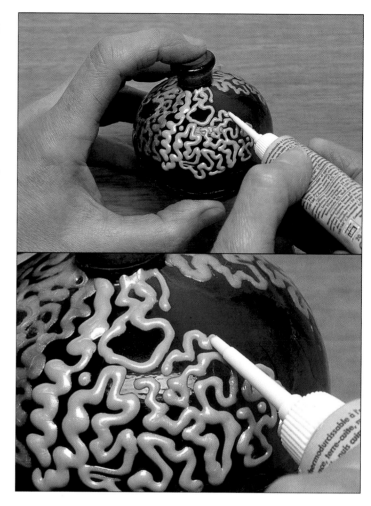

artist's tip

Practicing on a jam jar will help you to find a comfortable and accurate way of working on a round object and enable you to perfect your technique with the outliner. Collect practice jars to try out new effects.

3 Peel enough stickers off the backing sheet to fill the spaces on the bottle. Using tweezers, hold a sticker and add a dab of glass adhesive to its reverse. Turn the sticker over and carefully place it on the surface of the bottle in one of the open spaces in the gold design. Continue in this way until all the spaces are filled, then leave to dry.

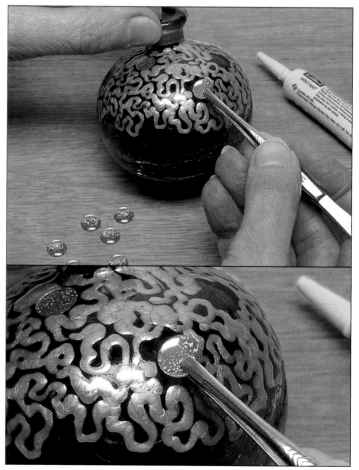

4 Using very little pressure on the tube of outliner, make a row of tiny gold dots around the lower edge of the design to complete the effect.

5 Decorate the top of the glass stopper with wiggly lines of gold outliner. Leave to dry until hard. Decorate other perfume bottles with variations of this technique. Tie an organdie ribbon bow or tassel around the neck of each one.

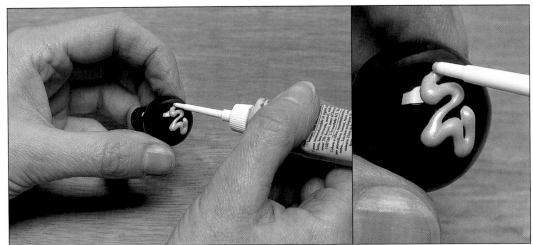

Alternative design:
Dots and Lines

Ribbed bottles are even easier to decorate with the gold outliner. Place the tip of the nozzle in the space between two ribs and draw it down carefully to form a thin line of gold. Make a row of tiny dots along the next space and then another line next to this. Continue in this way with alternate lines and dots until one side of the bottle is covered. Leave to dry, then decorate the other side to match.

Here the gold outliner design "grows" from the bottom upward, incorporating star-shaped stickers on turquoise glass for a vibrant, sumptuous effect.

Bottles and Vases
Gallery

Top shelf, left to right:

Rainbow Bottle
Inspired by a colorful organza ribbon seen in a craft shop, each section of the bottle was painted in a rainbow color to match the shades on the ribbon. Water-based paints or enamel paints would work equally well here.

Crazy Patchwork Style (Artist: Vicki Miller)
This is a fun way to paint glass. Start by drawing in the random design with dark colored outliner and leave to dry. Fill in the areas in alternating oil-based colors.

Frosted Glass
This looks great with shiny gold designs in freely waving lines and spirals using outliner or relief outliner.

Another Crazy Patchwork Design (Artist: Vikki Miller)
Use gold outliner combined with vivid pinks and purples for this effect.

Twin "Wavy" Bottles
Painted in matching stripes of black outliner and blue and yellow oil-based paints, these bottles are ideal for displaying a large bloom like a sunflower or a delphinium.

Blue and Pink Stripes
Wavy stripes of outliner decorate the neck of this elegant vase. A simple idea with stunning effect.

Perfect Patchwork (Artist: Vikki Miller)
The crazy patchwork technique has been perfected here with another design to tempt you into trying this easy but effective method.

Bottom shelf, left to right:

Bath Bottle
This unusually shaped bottle with a cork could be the perfect packaging for exotic bath or massage oil. Decorate it with a heart in colored outliner and give it to the one you love.

Blue and Green
Brush-paint this vase with water-based enamel paints in blending bands of blue and green. When dry, paint on meandering lines in gold to add highlights.

Trio of Stoppered Bottles (Artist: Vikki Miller)
Try any of these designs using vivid oil-based paints, such as Vitrail, and gold relief outliner.

Lidded Jar (Artist: Vikki Miller)
Paint this with yet more crazy patchwork in rich, dark shades of oil-based paint and gold relief outliner.

Glass-stoppered Bottle
The painted base which subtly floods color up the sides of the glass matches the brush-painted designs. Use water-based paints or enamel paints for this effect.

Tiny Glass Pots
Purely decorative pots were splodged with turquoise enamel paints on the outside and left to dry. Water-based gold paint was poured inside, swirled around and the excess tipped out to give the glass a golden lining.

Striped Bottles
Mask out stripes on frosted bottles and sponge them with water-based gold paint. The center bottle is striped with gold outliner and the third bottle left plain as a contrast.

4 Tumblers and Coasters

Frosted glass is easy to achieve and can be a modern, fashionable design solution for decorating plain glass. The frosting spray is fast to use, but remember that the items can only be hand-washed when decorated in this way.

You will need

blue glass etch spray
outliner in silver

Coasters made from
10 cm (4 in) square
pieces of 3 mm (about
¹⁄₁₆ in) thick glass with
ground edges
Plain tumblers
Plain paper (optional)
Tracing paper
Fine, black, waterproof
felt-tip pen
Acetate stencil sheet
(Mylar®)
Thick card or
cutting mat
Steel ruler
Craft knife
Stencil mount
Cardboard box to use
as a spraying booth
Glass etch spray, as
shown above
Outliner, such as
Porcelaine 150, as
shown above
Masking tape

1 Clean the coasters and tumblers thoroughly. Draw four 3 cm (1¼ in) squares in a grid about 1 cm apart on a piece of paper, or trace the squares on page 94 using the felt-tip pen. Lay the acetate over this template and draw over the squares with the felt-tip pen. Place the acetate on thick card or a cutting mat, then use the ruler and craft knife to cut out the squares. This makes a stencil for all the glasses and coasters.

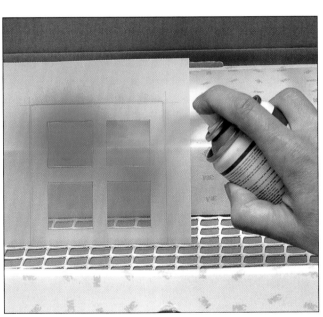

2 Spray the reverse of the stencil with stencil mount and leave for a few moments until it is tacky. Lay the stencil centrally onto one of the glass coasters and press in place. Place the coaster inside the spray booth. Shake the spraycan well, then spray the stencil with a fine coat of frosting and leave to dry. Repeat this process for one or two more coats, being careful not to spray too heavily or the liquid will run. When the final coat is touch-dry, lift off the stencil carefully. Repeat the process for all the coasters.

3 Use the same stencil to spray the design onto one side of one of the tumblers. Turn the tumbler upside down inside the spray booth to avoid getting the frosting spray inside the glass. You may need to trim some acetate off the stencil so that it matches the height of the glass. Spray as for the coasters and leave to dry.

4 Trace the designs in the template on page 94 using the felt-tip pen. Place the tracing under one of the frosted coasters. You can position the designs centrally inside the frosted squares or move them slightly to one side for a more unusual look.

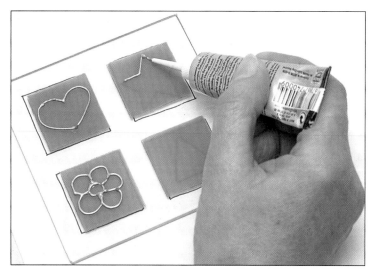

5 Using the silver outliner, follow the outlines of the designs underneath the glass to transfer the shapes to the surface. Take care not to smudge the silver paint as you are working. If this does occur, use the craft knife to scrape away the excess outliner before it dries hard.

artist's tip

Clean up any excess spray with a cotton bud dipped in mineral spirits or scrape off small specks with the tip of a craft knife.

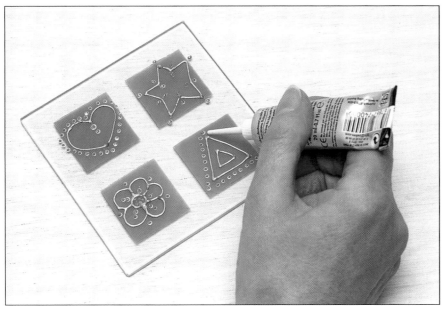

6 Finally, use the tip of the outliner nozzle to make tiny dots around the shapes. As the close-up shows, the dots can stray outside the frosted squares for a lively design. Leave the paint to dry for at least 24 hours until hard. Repeat on the remaining coasters and the tumblers. To trace the design onto the tumblers, fit the tracing paper inside the tumblers and hold it in place with masking tape.

Variation

Try blue outliner on some of the squares or silver on white-sprayed squares for a different look. You could also try different motifs such as letters, spirals or zigzags to develop this idea.

artist's tip

Always clean the glass well before you begin. To ensure the surface is completely free of grease, wipe over with a rag or kitchen paper soaked in denatured alcohol and leave to dry before decorating. This is important as it will ensure that the paints you are using will adhere to the glass properly.

ound pieces of glass can easily be transformed into
brilliant window decorations using dark outliner and
transparent glass paints. The light shining through them will
bring the vividly colored patterns to life and make colorful
shadows that enhance the simplest room. Virtually any design
will work sucessfully; these easy stained glass lightcatchers
are a good starting point.

You will need

turquoise
deep blue
yellow
crimson
outliner in Ming blue

Fine, black, waterproof
felt-tip pen
Tracing paper
Masking tape
Circles of glass, ready-
cut or cut to size
Outliner, such as
Porcelaine 150, as
shown above
Medium-sized
round brushes
Transparent
glass paints
Palette
Clear glass or
plastic beads
Glass bond adhesive
Clear household
adhesive
Narrow braid
Sticky tape
Thread to match braid
Appropriate thinner
for cleaning brushes

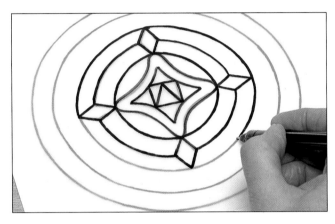

1 Clean the circle of glass thoroughly. Trace the template on page 94 onto a piece of tracing paper using the felt-tip pen.

2 Working on a clean flat surface, tape the glass circle over the tracing. Starting at the center of the design, use the outliner to follow the lines of the tracing. Turn the glass (and the paper underneath) as you work to enable you to keep the lines smooth and accurate. Leave the outliner to dry until hard.

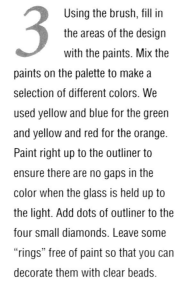

3 Using the brush, fill in the areas of the design with the paints. Mix the paints on the palette to make a selection of different colors. We used yellow and blue for the green and yellow and red for the orange. Paint right up to the outliner to ensure there are no gaps in the color when the glass is held up to the light. Add dots of outliner to the four small diamonds. Leave some "rings" free of paint so that you can decorate them with clear beads.

4 Pick up one of the beads in your fingertips and put a tiny dab of the glass adhesive on one side. Place the bead on the unpainted glass. Repeat this process until you have evenly spaced lines of beads on the areas of unpainted glass. Lay the lightcatcher flat in direct sunlight to harden the glue.

artist's tip

For easy hanging, you can buy circles of glass that already have a hole through which ribbon or yarn can be threaded.

5 Measure the braid to fit around the edge of the lightcatcher and add enough to the length to make a loop to hang the lightcatcher from. Wrap sticky tape around both ends of the measured length before cutting it, to prevent the strands unravelling. Lay the lightcatcher on scrap paper, run a thin line of household adhesive around its edge and place the braid around the edge with the center of the length of braid positioned at the bottom of the design and the loose ends at the top.

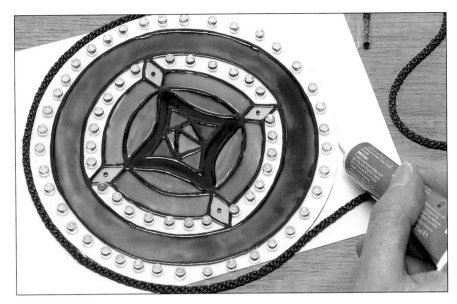

6 Slowly and carefully pull the braid tightly together at the top, then press it into position all round. Lift the lightcatcher off the paper so it does not stick, and leave to dry. Using matching thread, bind the braid together where it meets at the top of the lightcatcher. Carefully remove the sticky tape and seal each end of the braid with a dab of clear glue. Knot the ends together tightly to make a loop for hanging.

Variation

Use just the central area of the template on page 94 to make smaller lightcatchers. You could also choose a different combination of colors and thread large beads onto the braid for further decoration, or try a large and small lightcatcher strung above one another.

Glasses
Gallery

Top shelf, left to right:

Strawberry Glass
Adorning this elegant glass is a randomly stencilled
design using the templates on page 92, water-based
paints and a stencil brush. Stencil the red body of the
strawberry first and leave to dry. Stencil the leaves and
pips onto the strawberry in green.

Colored Squares
The pattern on this glass is painted with a square ended
brush and water-based paints in shades of blue and green
as an alternative to the rainbow glasses painted in the
same way on page 66.

Sundae Glass
This is decorated in a 1950s-inspired polka dot design in
two water-based colors. Perfectly round dots of a
uniform size are easily achieved by applying the paint
with the tip of of a cotton bud.

Zigzag Stripes
Another design inspired by the 1950s, these stripes are
drawn freehand with outliners in tourmaline pink, gold
and Ming blue.

Simple Carafe
This delicate blue glass carafe shows a simple design of
frosted brushstrokes around the top edge. Use a large,
round brush dipped in matte medium to create this quick
and easy design.

Bottom shelf, left to right:

Simple Tumbler
The pale blue tumbler matches the frosted brushstroke
design of the carafe on the top shelf.

Butterfly Tumbler
This tumbler with a molded design is beautifully
highlighted with the butterflies painted in red and yellow
oil-based paints. This is the perfect beginner's project.

Festive Brandy Glass (Artist: Vikki Miller)
Turn a plain brandy glass into an exciting and festive
vessel. Draw the star shapes in silver outliner and fill
in the centers of each star with oil-based paints in
pink and violet.

Venetian Effect
An exquisite Venetian-style wine glass can be created by
sponge-painting the lower part of the bowl of the glass
with water-based enamel paint in emerald. When this is
dry, sponge the top edge of the glass and the foot with
water-based gold paint.

Valentine Cocktail
Drink cocktails in style from a traditional cocktail glass
decorated with a red and gold heart. Draw the heart
shape in gold outliner and decorate with a row of tiny
gold dots, leave to dry and then paint the heart with
crimson oil-based paint. It's the ideal Valentine gift.

D ecorate these ultra-modern vases with colored gels that form a three-dimensional mix of iridescent shades and rich textures. Pattern and texture are built up on the outer surface of the vase, then left to dry to a hard finish that resembles molded glass.

You will need

iridescent green
opaline green
iridescent
ocean
iridescent silver
aquamarine
iridescent blue

Square tank vases
Gel paints, such as Gel
Crystal, as shown
Medium-sized flat
brush
Palette knife
Stiff card
Kitchen paper

1 Clean the vase thoroughly. To achieve the three-dimensional effect, work on one side of the vase and let it dry to a hard finish that won't smudge when you turn it over to work on the other side. Randomly squeeze some of the ocean gel near one edge of the vase. Using the brush, spread the gel out over most of the side of the vase.

2 Squeeze some of the darker blue gel near the lower edge of the vase. Using the palette knife, spread this out to form a uniform layer while merging some areas of the two colors together.

3 Build up the surface with aquamarine, using the palette knife as before. The sides of the vase can be decorated in the same way with a selection of the colors shown on page 43, or they can be further embellished, as shown opposite.

4 For a regular wave pattern, scrape through the gel with a comb cut from a piece of stiff card. Start at the top left-hand corner and pull the comb through the gel with a scalloping action. When you reach the right-hand side, lift off the comb and wipe away the excess gel with kitchen paper. Repeat this until the surface of the vase is covered with the wave texture. When you have completed one side of your vase, set it aside to dry, then repeat the process with the other three sides in turn.

Variation

Add glass nuggets as focal points in the textured surface. Use two or three nuggets in a random arrangement, choosing colors that complement the gels. Place each nugget on the surface of the wet gel, then push it down onto the surface of the glass without disturbing the surrounding gel. The gel will dry to form a neat seal that holds the nugget in place.

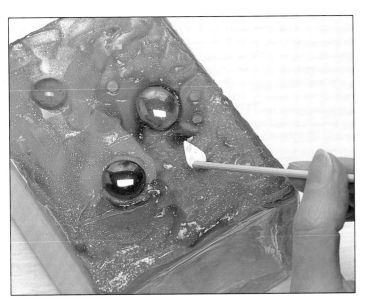

Clear acetate shapes can be added to create small windows in the gel. Use a hole-punch to cut out perfect circles of acetate or use scissors for larger shapes. Arrange the pieces of acetate on the surface of the wet gel, then use a cocktail stick or pencil to press them through the gel onto the surface of the glass. The rim of gel will hold the acetate in place.

The detail shows the dramatic effect of the combination of gels, glass nuggets and acetate. Try this technique on a night-light holder for a change.

painting glass/project 6

Glass-sided lamps that hold candles and night lights are perfect for summer dining on the patio or in a garden or conservatory. Decorate the plain glass to match garden cushions or crockery and create a colorful, glowing light source. The design works equally well on a round lamp and on one with straight glass sides.

You will need

turquoise
yellow
crimson

Hurricane lamp
Colored wax pencil
Narrow masking tape
Craft knife
Transparent
glass paints
Palette
Small pieces of
synthetic sponge
Relief outliner in silver
Appropriate thinner
for cleaning brushes

1 If you can remove the glass from the lamp it will be easier to work on it. Release the glass cylinder or the individual glass panels from the frame and clean thoroughly. Insert back into the frame, draw along the edge of the frame with a wax pencil as shown, so that you can easily see the area to be decorated, then remove again.

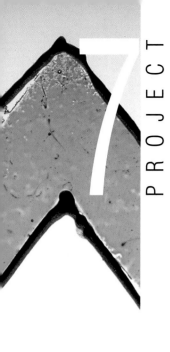

2 Measure and mark a central diamond shape on the glass with the wax pencil and mask it off with the masking tape. Then leave a gap and form an outer diamond border with another strip of tape. Use the craft knife to trim the tape into points where the ends overlap, then run your finger over the tape to make sure the edges adhere firmly to the glass.

artist's tip
You can use a hairdryer to speed up the drying time of the paints. Waft warm air over them for a few minutes – but do not concentrate the heat in one place for any length of time as this could cause damage.

3 Pour a little crimson paint into the palette and dip one side of a piece of sponge into the paint. Dab off the excess paint on the palette, then sponge the color onto the central diamond shape. Aim for an even coating without using too much paint which could seep under the masking tape.

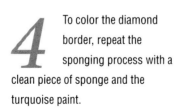

4 To color the diamond border, repeat the sponging process with a clean piece of sponge and the turquoise paint.

5 Sponge the outer area in the same way, using the yellow paint and a clean piece of sponge. Leave to dry. Carefully peel off the masking tape to reveal the finished pattern. If you have problems peeling it off cleanly, cut around the edge of the tape with the tip of the craft knife so that you slice through the layer of paint before removing the tape.

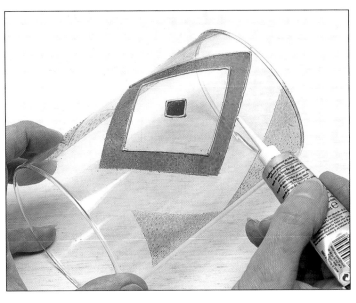

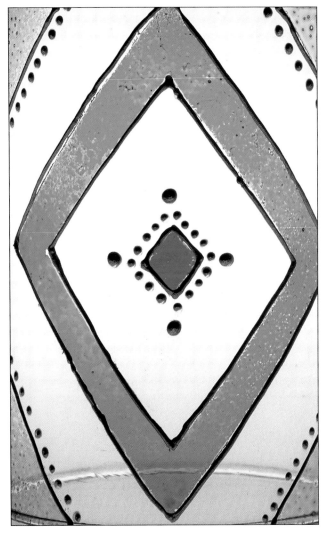

6 Trace the edge of each shape with the silver outliner. The outlines will emphasize the design and also cover any slight flaws on the edges of the paint.

7 Use the silver outliner to decorate the outline of the inner diamond and the inside of the diamond-shaped frame with rows of dots.

8 PROJECT Blue and Gold Glassware

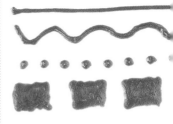

Hand-decorating a random collection of dark blue glass makes a spectacular set reminiscent of expensive Venetian glassware. This simple design with its richly contrasting colors has maximum impact. With a little practice, squeezing the outliner through the nozzle will produce pleasing results that require very little artistic skill.

You will need

outliner in gold

Blue wine glasses,
tumblers and empty
mineral water bottle
Masking tape
Ruler
Pencil
Outliner, as
shown above
Plastic-topped cork
that fits the bottle
(optional)

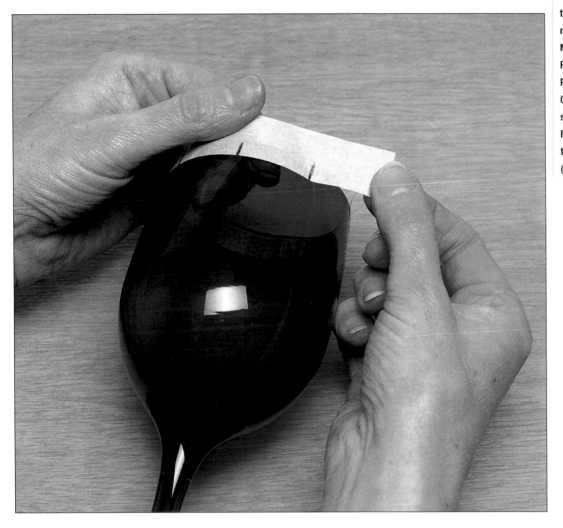

1 Clean the glassware thoroughly. Wrap a piece of masking tape around the top of one of the wine glasses and trim it to the circumference of the rim. Remove the tape and place it on the work surface. Use the ruler to divide the strip of masking tape into eight equal sections and mark these with the pencil along the lower edge. Replace the tape round the top edge of the glass.

2 Use the gold outliner to draw diamond shapes onto the glass. The top point of each diamond should match up with the marks on the tape. Start with the outline of the diamond, then spiral in toward the center to fill the shape with gold.

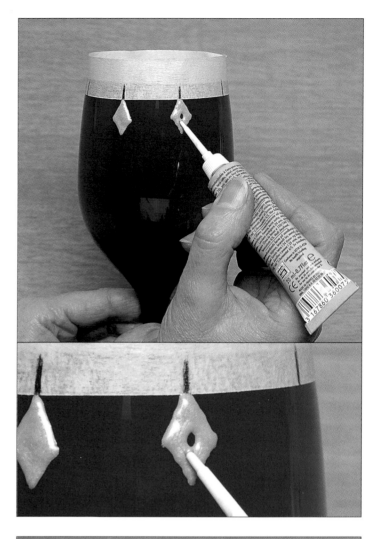

3 Make a large dot centrally between each diamond, using the gold outliner. Then go around the glass again adding four small dots around each large dot.

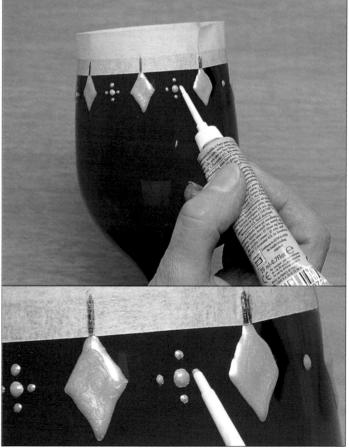

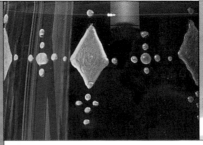

4 Carefully remove the masking tape from the glass. (You can use it again on a matching glass.) Make four dots around each diamond, using the gold outliner, then add four dots below each diamond. Decorate the foot of the wine glass with rows of gold dots. Repeat the process with the remaining wine glasses.

5 Follow the same method for the bottle and tumblers and decorate them with similar gold diamonds and dots. Wrap masking tape around the bottle and divide it into equal sections to position the diamonds.

6 If you wish to make a stopper for the bottle, decorate a plastic-topped cork from a sherry or port bottle with lines and dots of gold outliner. When all the glassware has been decorated, bake it in the oven (omitting the plastic-topped cork) following the manufacturer's instructions.

artist's tip

If you want to draw an accurate pattern for a more complex design using conical tumblers, make a paper template by rolling the glass across a sheet of paper. As you do this, draw a line that follows the top and bottom edges of the glass. Cut the shape out, wrap it around the glass and trim the ends of the paper so that it fits into the glass exactly. You can now use this to create more adventurous repeat patterns to trace onto the glass itself.

Flora and Fauna
Gallery

Top shelf, left to right:

Stoppered Bottles (Artist: Annette Malbon)
All these bottles are decorated using outliner and paints which the artist mixes herself from pigment and transparent base paints to achieve a wide range of vibrant colors.

Vine Jug (Artist: Vikki Miller)
The jug is decorated with an impressive grape vine motif. This should be drawn in black outliner from a tracing taped to the inside of the jug and then painted in rich colors.

Color Combinations (Artist: Vikki Miller)
This floral vase is painted with simple hand-drawn black outlines which are then filled in with a small brush, using alternating oil-based colors.

Bright Dots
The flower centers and the entire design on the blue and yellow jug were created by dipping cotton buds into paint and dabbing them onto the glass to make perfect dots each time.

Bottom shelf, left to right:

Stemmed Glass (Artist: Annette Malbon)
This delicate blue-and-pink flower pattern suits the shape and color of the glass. Look around and let yourself be inspired by the glassware you find, as this artist does.

Ducks and Frogs (Artist: Annette Malbon)
Outliner and bright green and yellow paints were used to create the jolly designs on these glasses. You could use different designs and colors to customize glasses for seasonal or other special occasions.

Perfect Petals
The wide petals on the glass are made with a round brush used flat on to the glass. The thinner petals on the jug (far right) were painted using only the tip of an angled brush.

Bold Bloom
A bold jungle flower is first drawn in black outliner and then filled with vivid pink and violet. The leaves are painted in emerald paint to create this exotic glass.

Two-tone Jar (Artist: Vikki Miller)
This is painted using the same technique as the small floral vase above.

Candle and Tea-light Holders

Plain glass candle and tea-light holders can be turned into elegant, bejewelled creations that would grace the smartest dining table. The larger candle holder is embellished with glass nuggets in rich jewel colors, while smaller "jewels" are simply painted onto the tea-light holders.

Safety note: Never leave lighted candles unattended.

You will need

crimson
turquoise
emerald
lemon
gold
outliner in gold

Clear glass candle
holder and tea-light
holders
Narrow masking tape
Water-based paint,
such as Porcelaine
150, as shown above
Palette
Small pieces of
synthetic sponge
Outliner, as
shown above
Glass bond adhesive
Glass nuggets in
jewel colors
Small round brush
Masking fluid
Transparent paints
in jewel colors

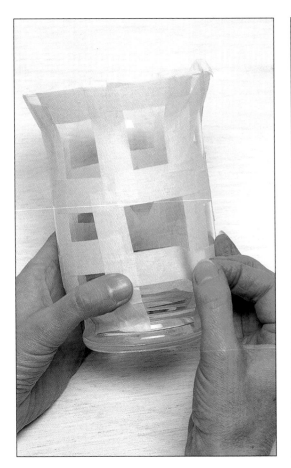

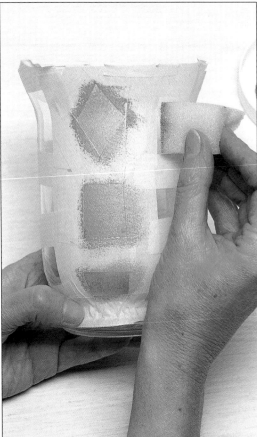

1 Clean the holders thoroughly. Use strips of masking tape to mask a pattern of squares, diamonds and rectangles all around the candle holder. Arrange the shapes vertically in groups, with about three shapes in each group.

2 Pour some gold paint onto the palette and dip a piece of sponge into it. Dab off any excess paint on the palette, then sponge the color onto the masked shapes. Leave to dry, then apply a second coat for maximum coverage.

3 Remove the masking tape. Using gold outliner, draw lines around both sides of each shape, linking the shapes in each vertical group. Work carefully to avoid smudging the paint. Leave to dry until hard.

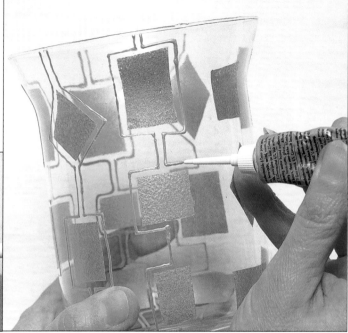

4 Finally, use the glass glue to stick the nuggets onto some of the gold shapes. Work with the candle holder flat on the work surface and leave each nugget in the sunlight until the glue is dry before turning the holder to work on the next one. This will prevent the nuggets slipping off while the glue is wet.

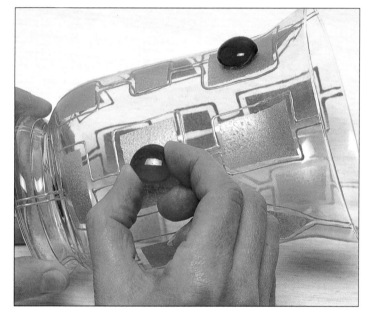

5 For the tea-light holders, use strips of masking tape to mask about five shapes around each holder. Using the brush, paint a circle of the masking fluid in the center of each shape. Leave to dry.

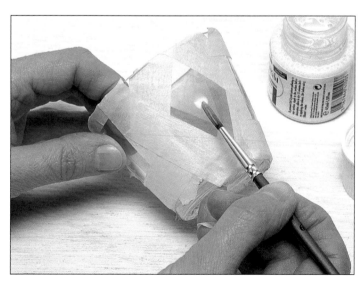

6 Sponge the shapes with one or two coats of gold paint, as in step 2, and leave to dry completely.

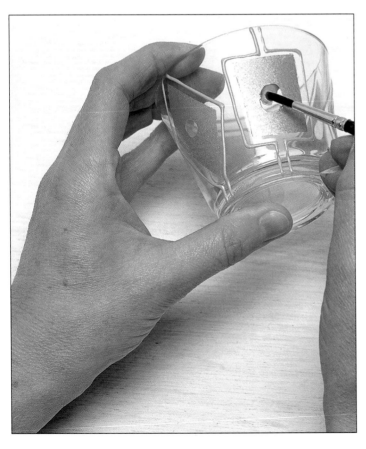

7 Remove the tape and draw gold outlines, as in step 3. Leave to dry completely, then rub the masking fluid off the center of the gold shapes with your fingertip. Bake the candle holder and tea-light holders in the oven following the manufacturer's instructions. Paint the central circles inside the gold shapes on the tea-light holders with the jewel-colored paints, then leave to dry.

artist's tip

If you wish to add color to an item, paint the base with a glass paint. If the glass is quite thick the color will reflect up the sides without adding to the pattern or spoiling the design.

Swedish-style
Wine Glasses

Delicate, classic designs are stencilled and painted onto simple wine glasses in a charming Swedish style. Although the technique is subtle, it is very effective and can be adapted and used on many different-shaped glasses, jugs and decanters.

You will need

matte medium

Acetate stencil sheet
(Mylar®)
Fine, black, waterproof
felt-tip pen
Thick card or
cutting mat
Craft knife
Plain wine glasses
Pencil
Stencil mount
Matte medium,
as shown
Palette or small dish
Small stencil brush
Small round brush

1 Clean the glasses thoroughly. Cut two squares of acetate and use the felt-tip pen to trace the templates on page 92 onto them. Place the acetate on the thick card or a cutting mat, then use the craft knife to cut out the designs. This makes the stencils for the large and small motifs.

2 Hold the stencil for the large motif in position on one of the wine glasses. Ensure the central line is vertical, then use the pencil to draw a line on the stencil that follows the rim of the wine glass. This will help you to position the design accurately on the glass.

3 Spray the reverse of the stencil with stencil mount, then leave to dry until tacky. The adhesive will hold the stencil in position on the shiny, curved surface of the glass while you work.

4 Position the stencil on the glass, lining up the pencil line with the rim of the glass. Pour a little matte medium onto a dish and dip the tip of the stencil brush into it. Dab off the excess on scrap paper, then dab a thin coat of the medium over the stencil. Leave to dry for a few moments, then peel off the stencil. Stencil the other glasses in the same way.

5 Prepare the stencil for the small motif, as in step 3. When the large motif is quite dry, stencil small motifs around the rest of the rim of the wine glass, spacing them evenly. Leave to dry. Stencil the other glasses in the same way.

artist's tip

If medium (or paint) accidentally seeps under a stencil, wait until it is touch-dry and then use the tip of a craft knife to carefully scrape away the excess. When you have corrected the shapes, leave the glasses until the medium is completely dry, then bake them in the oven following the manufacturer's instructions.

6 Using the small brush, paint small dots of the medium onto the glasses to link the stencilled motifs. Leave to dry, then bake in the oven following the manufacturer's instructions.

Lightcatchers
Gallery

This page:

Christmas Decorations
Small triangles of glass were painted with transparent colors inside gold outlines. Trees and stars are simple to do and you can choose a color scheme to go with the rest of your decorations. Glue narrow braid around the edge of each triangle when it is dry and make loops to hang them from festive garlands, at the window or from the branches of the Christmas tree.

Opposite page:

Hearts, Stars and Abstract Patterns
Most of these lightcatchers are made using the same basic method as shown on page 37-39. Start with a traced outline design which is drawn onto the glass using outliner in black, dark grey or a different color. When this is dry, paint each area in a different color using a selection of transparent paints.

Pale Shades
To achieve a different effect, as on the lightcatcher with the pale blue pattern (center), first sponge through a stencil and outline the design later.

Fairytale on Glass (Artist: Sue McIldowie)
The large lightcatcher with the complex design is decorated with flowers, fruit and birds, ideal for a child's room. Hang it from the window to show off the wonderfully vivid colors and fairytale design.

All the lightcatchers are hung up with braid glued around the edge or thread looped through a hole in the top.

imple but effective, this easy technique, combined with stunning colors, makes a set of glasses and dishes that would be great for a children's party or a summer dining table. The mosaic-like squares are painted with a single brush stroke and the rainbow colors can be adapted to go with your decor. The molded lines on the glasses used in this project help to keep the squares level, but the decoration can just as easily be painted freehand.

You will need

Ming blue
citrine
Parma violet
saffron
turquoise
coral
emerald
ruby

**Glasses, fruit bowls
and jug**
**Water-based paints,
such as Porcelaine
150, as shown above**
Small flat brush
**Spare piece of glass
to practice on**
**Medium-sized
flat brush**

1 Clean the glasses thoroughly. Arrange the paints in the order in which you will use them, remembering how one color leads on to the next in a rainbow. Start with emerald, then turquoise, blue, Parma violet, ruby, coral, saffron and citrine.

2 Using the small, flat brush, try painting even squares on a spare piece of glass by making a single short brush stroke for each one. Then, starting with emerald, paint evenly spaced squares diagonally around the base of one of the glasses. Leave to dry while you paint the next glass in the same way. Repeat the process with all the glasses.

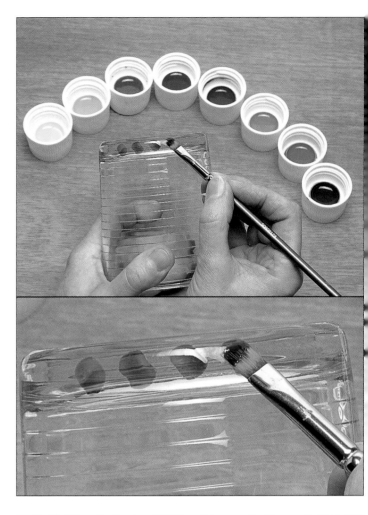

3 Working on the first glass again, use the same brush to make a row of squares with the turquoise paint. Make each square fit under the space between the squares in the emerald row. Finish this row and repeat with the remaining glasses.

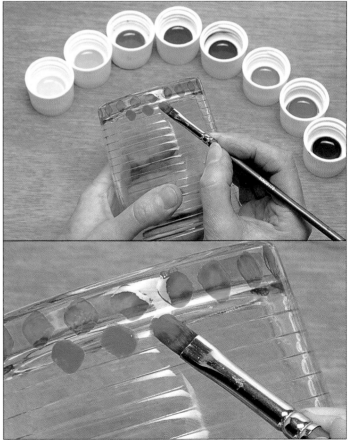

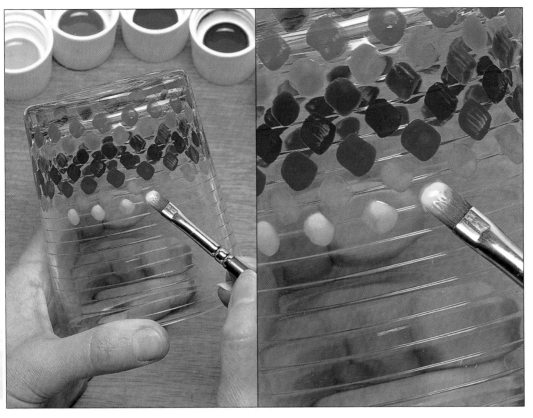

4
Continue in this way with each color, finishing with a row of citrine squares about halfway up each glass. Paint the fruit bowls and jug to complete the set. The jug is bigger than the other items, so use the medium-sized brush in order to make larger brush strokes. Leave all the glassware to dry for 24 hours, then bake in the oven following the manufacturer's instructions.

Variation

Use a different palette of colors, perhaps to team with patterned china and table linen.

artist's tip

Another way to add interest to uncolored glass is to paint into any cut areas. The thick base of this glass has a star pattern and has been painted in alternate shades of blue and green. This could be left as the sole decoration or combined with other patterns in harmonizing colors. Use a small, pointed brush to reach into the indentations, then wipe across the surface to remove any excess paint and leave clean edges.

T his salad set has a summery look and a charmingly hand-painted finish. The life-like daisies are very easy to paint using angled brushes to form the regular and naturalistic petals with single strokes. Dividing the plate and bowl into equal sections means you won't need to draw a pattern for this delightful design.

You will need

citrine
ivory white
malachite

Glass plates and salad bowl
Small square brush
Water-based paints, such as Porcelaine 150, as shown above
Colored wax pencil
Ruler
Medium-sized round brush
Medium-sized angled brush
Piece of glass or acetate to practice on
Long-haired brush
Small angled brush
Cotton buds
Denatured alcohol

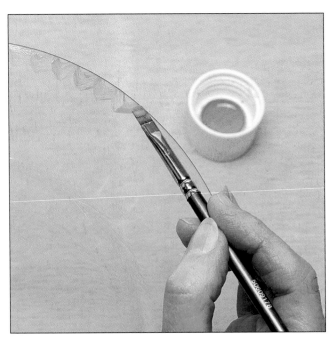

1 Clean the plates and bowl thoroughly. Using the small square brush and malachite, paint an even zigzag border around the edge of one of the plates. Make about three zigzags, then replenish the paint on the brush to keep the color even. If you make a mistake or the pattern becomes uneven, wipe it off quickly with a damp cloth. Leave to dry. Paint the remaining plates in the same way.

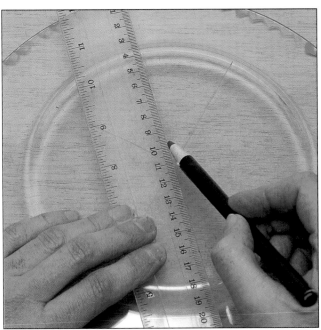

2 Using the wax pencil and the ruler, draw across the center of the first plate to divide it in half. Repeat the process to divide it into quarters and then eighths. The lines will help you to space the flowers evenly.

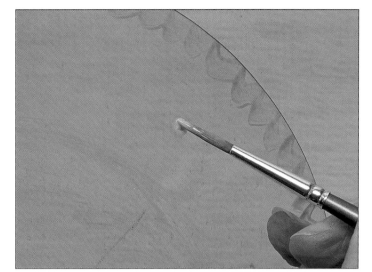

3 Using the medium-sized round brush and the citrine color, paint a solid circle level with the end of each line to form the flower centers. Paint each circle centrally on the raised edge of the plate to leave space around it for the petals. Leave to dry while you paint the remaining plates.

4 Using the white paint and medium-sized angled brush, practice painting the flower petals on a spare piece of glass or acetate. Dip just the tip of the brush into the paint, then place it on the glass with a single short dabbing motion. This will make a convincing petal shape each time and you should be able to paint two or three petals with one dip into the paint. The fullness and shape of the petals will vary according to the pressure you put on the brush.

5 Now paint the daisy petals onto the first plate. Put the first four petals opposite each other, turning the plate so that the point of the brush is always closest to the flower center. Then paint two petals in each gap. Continue in this way until you have eight complete daisies. Try to keep them the same size with the petals evenly spaced. Leave to dry while you paint the petals onto the remaining plates.

6 Working on the first plate, use the malachite paint and the long-haired brush to paint a linking stem between each daisy. Work from the inner to the outer edge of the plate and make the line curve naturally in a gentle S-shape. Turn the plate as you go so that you are always working from the outer edge of the plate. Use the same paint and brush to paint two short branches on each stem.

7 Go over the branches with a second coat of malachite if the original lines seem too pale.

artist's tip

If you find it difficult to keep your hand steady when painting on curved surfaces and larger objects like the salad bowl, rest it on a small box so that it is on the same level as the surface you are working on. You can also use pieces of kneadable adhesive to hold the object in place.

8 Paint about ten small leaves around each branch, following the technique described in step 5 but using the small angled brush and malachite paint. Always point the brush towards the stem so that the leaves are the same shape. Paint the stems, branches and leaves onto the remaining plates, then decorate the salad bowl. Divide its base into sections, as in step 2, then extend the lines to the rim of the bowl and decorate in the same way as the plates. Leave the plates and bowl to dry, then remove the wax pencil marks with a cotton bud dipped in denatured alcohol. Bake in the oven following the manufacturer's instructions.

Each stroke made with an angled brush makes a single, very natural-looking petal or leaf shape. Try a similar design with multicolored flowers that look like gerberas rather than daisies.

Mirrors, Frames and Candle Holders
Gallery

This page:

Glass paints are ideal for adding a decorative, painted edging to plain glass or a mirror.

Beaded Mirror
The round mirror shown here was masked using the template on page 92 to create a wavy edge sprayed with frosting. The edging is decorated with glued-on glass nuggets drizzled with silver outliner.

Fabulous Frames
The pictures are mounted in inexpensive clip frames decorated with patterns drawn in outliner to create a frame effect. Black and silver was used to decorate the smaller frame. The larger one has a black grid with tourmaline pink detailing. When the outliner had dried, some areas were painted with deep blue transparent paint to complete the design and complement the picture.

Opposite page:

Candleholders are perfect for small beginner projects and make lovely gifts. They also sell very well at craft fairs and fundraising events.

Flower Light
The flower-shaped holder is adorned with glued-on glass nuggets in matching colors and drizzled with gold outliner.

Colorful Stars
The round candleholder was masked with self-adhesive stars and sprayed with frosting. Once the masks are peeled off, colour in the clear star shapes with oil-based paints.

Swirls and Dots
Freehand lines, dots and spirals in gold outliner give a lovely effect on colored glass.

U se subtly colored porcelain paints to create an ancient Roman look for a vase. You will totally transform the surface of the glass so that it resembles an ancient, blue-green opaline finish, shaded with pewter and gold.

You will need

gold
pewter
turquoise
opaline green

Clear or pale-colored
glass vase in a
classic shape
Water-based paints,
such as Porcelaine
150, as shown above
Palette
Piece of glass or
acetate to practice on
Small pieces of
synthetic sponge

1 Clean the vase thoroughly. Spread the paints onto a palette and, starting at the top edge of the vase, sponge on some of the opaline green onto one side of the vase, working down toward the base. Add some of the turquoise near the rim and blend it carefully with the lighter color. The small bubbles that appear on the surface will dry to create the texture needed. Set the vase aside until touch-dry, then paint the other side. Leave until touch-dry.

artist's tip
Use this technique
with different
colors as the base
for an opulent gold
or silver design
similar to Venetian
glassware.
Terracotta mixed
with copper, or
pinks with a pearl
finish would look
particularly good.

2 Experiment with the
different shades on a
spare piece of glass or
acetate. Use small pieces of
synthetic sponge to apply the
colors with a firm dabbing motion
and blend them together as you
work around the vase.

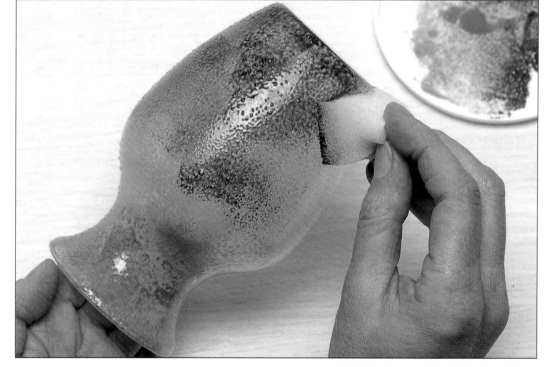

3 Turn the vase around again and sponge a light
coating of pewter around the base, shading it
up the sides. Blend this with some of the blue-
green so that the colors merge. Leave until touch-dry.

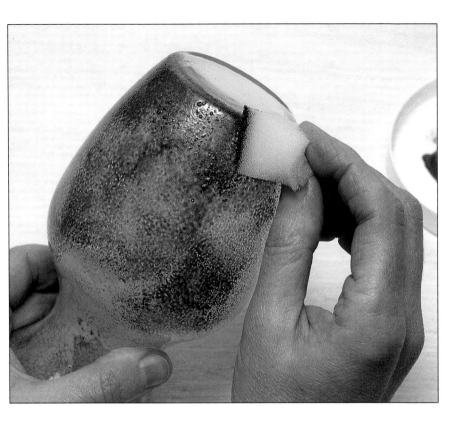

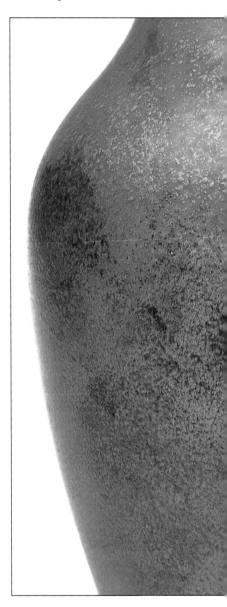

Try to achieve perfect blending of the blues and greens for best results.

4 Using a clean piece of sponge, add some more pewter color near the base of the vase to darken it and accentuate the metallic finish. Leave until touch-dry.

5 Pour a little gold paint onto a clean palette. Using a clean piece of sponge, add subtle gold highlights over the blue-green areas, concentrating the color on the shoulder and rim of the vase. Leave to dry completely. Bake in the oven following the manufacturer's instructions.

arge, plain glass beads are reasonably priced and fun to decorate. You can easily produce hand-colored ones to match your fabric, and they will cost a fraction of what you would pay in a shop. When you have painted a collection of beads with different designs, thread them together to create a highly individual, beaded fringe that will catch the light and make the colors glow. Simple spots and stripes are very effective while marbled and dipped versions also look good.

You will need

emerald
green-gold
lemon
turquoise
dark blue
yellow

Large oval glass beads
Large flat glass beads
Smaller round
glass beads
Wooden skewers
Masking tape
Transparent glass
paints, as shown above
Long-haired brushes
Small round brushes
or cotton buds
Appropriate thinner
for cleaning brushes
Jar filled with sand
Large darning needle
Embroidery yarn or
fine cord
Fabric blind to decorate

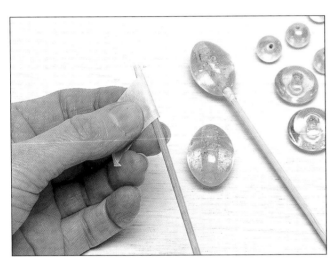

1 Clean the beads thoroughly. Push each bead onto a wooden skewer. The skewer will hold the bead so that you don't smudge the paint as you work. If the hole in the bead is too large, wind some masking tape around the top of the skewer to make it big enough to hold the bead firmly in place.

2 For a one-color bead, simply dip it into the pot of paint and lift it out quickly. Allow any drops of paint to fall back into the pot, then leave the bead to dry on the skewer. Decorate some of the large beads in this way and all of the small ones. You can also create half-colored beads by dipping them halfway into the paint.

3 Use the long-haired brush to paint even stripes on a selection of large beads. Coat the brush well with the paint, rest the tip of the brush on the widest point of the bead and then twist the skewer until the paint forms a stripe all around the middle. Leave to dry.

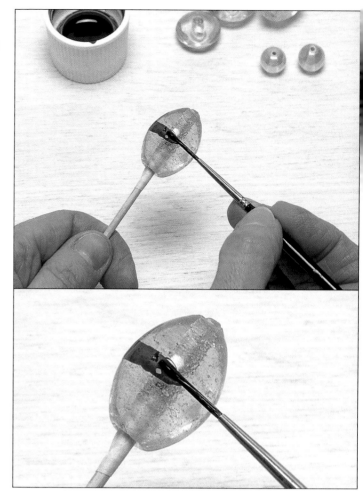

4 Paint dots of all sizes on other large beads, using a small round brush or a cotton bud. You can paint them directly onto unpainted beads or add lines of dots to half-colored and striped designs once the paint has dried. Try dark contrasting dots on a bead dipped in a paler color. Leave all the beads to dry.

Variation

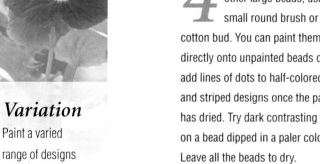

Paint a varied range of designs and colors to make a lively and interesting fringe for a lampshade.

5 To avoid smudging the wet paint, push the ends of the skewers into a jar filled with sand. This will hold the beads securely while the paint dries and enables you to view the range of colors and designs.

6 To make the beads into a fringe for the blind, use the large darning needle to thread a few beads onto embroidery yarn or fine cord. Then thread on a small bead and take the yarn back through the other beads. With the needle still threaded, stitch both ends of the yarn into the back of the bottom edge of the blind. Knot the ends of the yarn together and trim them neatly. Make a fringe in this way, spacing the rows of beads evenly and varying the beads in each row.

painting glass/project 14

Plates & Bowls
Gallery

This page:

Plates are fun to decorate as their flat surfaces are easy to paint on. Try a single design as a decorative piece for display, or paint a whole set for a special table setting.

Blue Frost
The blue frosted plate is decorated with matching glass nuggets glued evenly around the edge of the plate using glass bond. The area between each nugget is decorated with random, wavy lines of gold outliner.

Marble Effect
The random mottled design on the underside of the plate is achieved using the marbling technique on page 16. Dark blue and violet oil-based paints blend well together using this method.

Eastern Flavor
For the oriental design, tape a tracing of the characters on page 94 to the underside of the plate and follow the designs in black outliner on the surface of the plate. When dry, fill in with black water-based paint. Leave to dry and then sponge the underside of the plate's edge using gold water-based paint. Bake in the oven to make the design permanent.

Opposite page:

All the bowls are painted with oil-based paints and so can only be used as decorative pieces.

Molded Swirls
Simply fill in the smooth surface around the molded pattern with chartreuse green and leave the molded lines clear.

Fish Bowl (Artist: Vikki Miller)
The different fish shapes are painted freehand with oil-based paints in various colors. You can also draw your designs on paper, tape them inside the bowl and trace them with black outliner.

Marbled Bowls
These two bowls were marbled following the instructions on page 16. Once dry, they were decorated with some gold sponging around the top edge and a "shoreline" of gold outliner.

Flat Fish
The fins and scales on this molded fish dish were painted with a mix of blues and greens, to make a pretty dish for the bathroom.

Art Deco
Uplight

rt Deco is a classic, simple style that is ideal for this angular uplight. Soft, muted colors with black and frosted finishes provide an authentic look that is redolent of the 1930s. The shade can be made of clear plastic instead of glass, but remember that plastic cannot be baked in the oven as it will melt.

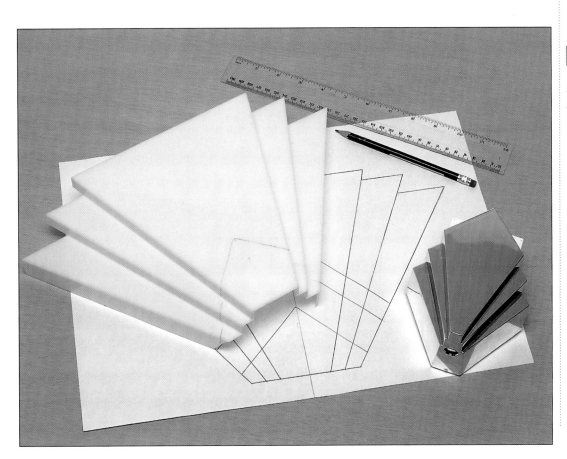

1 Clean the shade thoroughly. Mark the top edge of the holder on the shade with the wax pencil and then remove the holder. Trace the outline of the shade onto a sheet of paper. Draw the fan sections and an inverted V-shaped stripe on paper as shown, using ruler and pencil.

2 Measure and mark a central line on the shade using the ruler and wax pencil. Using the design you drew in step 1 as a guide, measure and mark the top point of the V-shaped stripe on this line.

3 Starting at the marked point on the central line, press a strip of masking tape out toward the left-hand edge of the shade. Repeat this on the other side to form an inverted V. Press the tape firmly into any indentations to keep the line straight, and run your finger over the edges of the tape to ensure the paint will not seep underneath it.

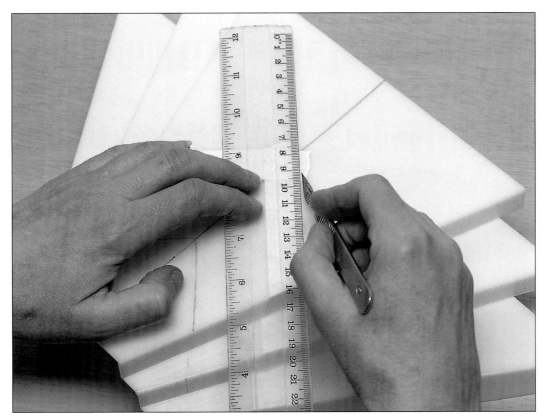

4 Using the ruler and craft knife, trim the masking tape into an accurate point where the layers overlap. Peel off the excess tape.

5 Leave a gap about twice the width of the masking tape, then apply two strips of tape, as in step 3, to make the top of the V. Remove the wax pencil mark with a cotton bud dipped in denatured alcohol. Pour a little of each color onto the palette and mix some opaline green with a little anthracite and ivory white to make a pale greeny-grey. Use this color and the fan-shaped brush to fill in the areas at the top of the shade and the top part of the inverted V-shape at the base. Dab the brush flat onto the surface of the shade, starting at the top in each area, and gradually work out from the center with a dabbing motion to make a regular, scalloped texture.

6 Mix some of the lapis blue paint with the ivory white to make a pale blue and apply this in the same way to the middle stripe. Leave to dry.

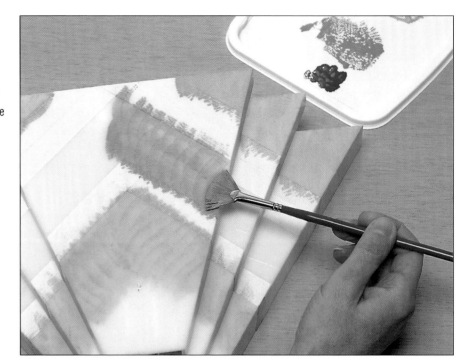

7 Carefully peel off the masking tape to reveal the painted stripes. If the tape starts to pull off the paint in some places, run the tip of the craft knife along its edge to cut through the layer of paint, then peel off the tape.

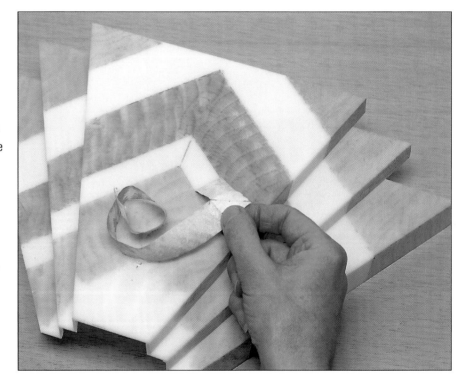

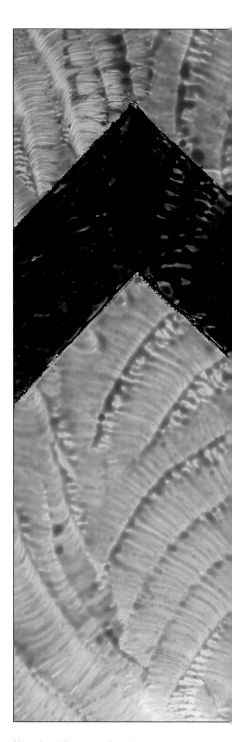

8 Rub out the remainder of the wax pencil line with a cotton bud dipped in denatured alcohol. When the paint is completely dry, lightly press strips of masking tape onto either side of the unpainted stripe in the center of the shade, following the instructions in step 3.

Note the delicate, scalloped texture achieved with the fan-shaped brush. For perfect results, practice the dabbing motion necessary to create this effect on a piece of spare glass or acetate.

9 Paint the central stripe with the anthracite color and fan-shaped brush, using the dabbing technique described in step 5 to create a scalloped texture. Leave to dry, then peel off the tape as in step 7. Bake in the oven, following the manufacturer's instructions, but only if you have used a glass – and not a plastic – shade. Attach the holder to the uplight.

Templates

Strawberry Glass
Red stencil
(see page 40)

Swedish-style
Wine Glasses
(see page 60)

Strawberry Glass
Green stencil
(see page 40)

Beaded Mirror
(see page 74)
Enlarge to fit
your mirror size

Lightcatchers
(see pages 64-65)

Lightcatcher
(see page 36)

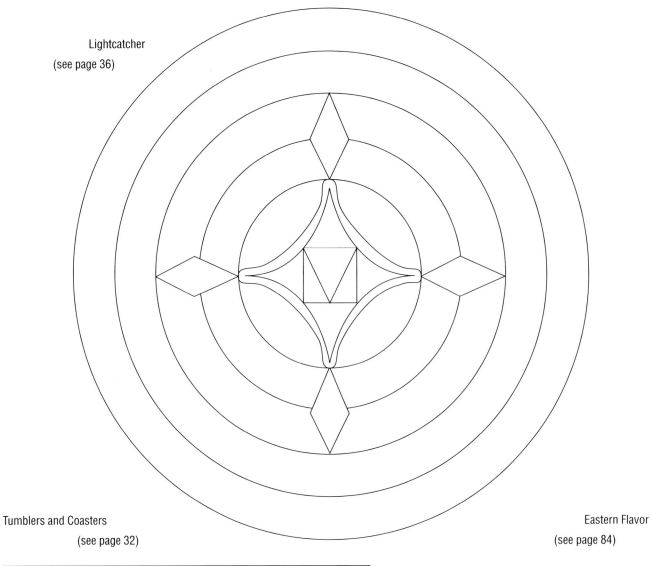

Tumblers and Coasters

(see page 32)

Eastern Flavor

(see page 84)

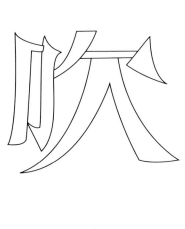

Suppliers and Acknowledgements

DecoArt
Box 386
Hwy Jct 150 & 27
Stanford, KY 40484
www.decoart.com
(800) 367-3047
(paint supplier)

Delta Technical Coatings
2550 Pellissier Pl
Whittier, CA 90601
www.deltacrafts.com
(800) 423-4135
(paint supplier)

Gem Craft, Inc.
1590 NW 159th Street
Miami, FL 33169
1-800-627-0820
(paint supplier)

Pebeo of America
Rt. 78, Airport Rd
Swanton, BT 05488
(819) 829-5012
www.pebeo.com
(paint supplier)

Plaid Enterprises, Inc.
P.O. Box 7600
Norcross, GA 30091-7600
1-800-842-4197
www.plaidonline.com
(paint supplier)

ACKNOWLEDGEMENTS

Many thanks to John Wright of
Pebeo UK for the generous supply of
different paints and outliners that have
been used extensively in this book and to
Carol Hook of Clear Communications Ltd
for all her help and information on the
products provided.
Also grateful thanks to Sue McIldowie,
Vikki Miller and Annette Malbon for
allowing me to show some of their glass
painting work in the gallery sections of
the book.

Index

3-dimensional effect/texture 16, 42

A
abstract pattern (moulded) 21
acetate
    shapes 45
    stencil 60
Art Deco uplighter 86

B
baking
    outliners *see* water-based paints
    water-based paints 10-12
Beaded blind 80
blending colors 13, 14
Blue and gold glassware 50
Bottles and vases gallery 30
bowls 84-85
brushes 8
    angled 13
    cleaning 10, 12
    fan-shaped 13, 89
    flat 13
    long-haired 13
    round 13

C
Candle and tea-light holders 56
candle holders 74-75
chinagraph (wax) pencil 10
Christmas decorations 64
cleaning
    brushes 10, 24
    glassware 8
    grease off glass 8, 27
    natural sponges 14
cocktail sticks/wooden skewers 10
color schemes 17
comb (for patterns) 44
cotton buds 10
crackle finish 16
craft knife 10
crazy patchwork 30

D
denatured alcohol 8
design inspiration 17

E
edging 13, 74
embedding (into gel paints) 12
excess (removing)
    paint 63
    spray 34

F
Flora and fauna gallery 54
Flowery salad plates and bowl 70
foam applicator 14
frames 74
frosted colors 12
frosted (etched) designs 15, 32, 84
frosting spray 12

G
gel, using 16
    as glue 16
gel paints 12
glass adhesive 16, 38
glass beads 80
glass cutter 10
Glasses gallery 40
glass nuggets 16, 45, 58, 74, 84
glassware
    baking/firing 10-12
    for painting 8
glue gun 16

H
hanging
    lightcatchers 29, 64
    night-light holders 25
Hurricane Lamp 46

I
inspiration 17

L
labels, removing sticky residue 22
leaves 13, 54
Lightcatchers 36
Lightcatchers gallery 64
lining (with color) 30

M
marbling 16, 84, 85
masking 15
masking fluid 58
masking tape 10, 15, 48, 50, 57, 88
matte
    finish 10
    medium 12, 15, 40, 62
    varnish 12
metallic finish 79
mineral spirits 12
Mirrors, frames and candle holders 74
mixing paints 24
    with thinners 25
molded designs 19, 40, 84-85
Molded bottles and jars 18

O
oil-based paints 10
outliners 12, 27, 50
    using 15

P
pastel effect 12
Perfume Bottles 26
petals 13, 54, 70-72
plant stems and tendrils 13, 21, 73
Plates and bowls gallery 84
practice jars 28

R
Rainbow jug, tumblers and bowls 66
relief outliners *see* outliners
Roman vase 76

S
scratching designs 15
solvents 8
spatulas 10
sponges 10
    natural 13
    synthetic 14
sponging 48-48, 57, 77-79
Square Flower Vases 42
Stained Glass Night Lights 22
stencilling 12, 14, 40, 60-63
Swedish-style wine glasses 60

T
templates, making 53
texture 12, 13, 14, 42-44, 89, 91
Tiffany glass effect 12
Tumblers and coasters 32

V
Venetian style 40, 50, 78

W
water-based enamel paints 12
water-based paints 10
    firing/baking 10-12
wave pattern 44
wax pencil see Chinagraph pen